WIVES OF THE SAME SCHOOL

Tributes and Straight Talk

Deji Badiru

WIVES OF THE SAME SCHOOL
TRIBUTES AND STRAIGHT TALK

iUniverse books may be ordered through booksellers or by contacting:

iUniverse
1663 Liberty Drive
Bloomington, IN 47403
www.iuniverse.com
1-800-Authors (1-800-288-4677)

ISBN: 978-1-5320-7719-7 (sc)
ISBN: 978-1-5320-7720-3 (e)

Library of Congress Control Number: 2019943809

Print information available on the last page.

iUniverse rev. date: 06/18/2019

Adedeji Badiru writes as the primary author for ABICS Publications (www. abicspublications.com), A Division of AB International Consulting Services, dedicated to books for home, work, and leisure.

ABICS Publications

A Division of
AB International Consulting Services (ABICS)
www.ABICSPublications.com
Books for home, work, and leisure

Adedeji's book series, published by iUniverse, Inc., on recreational, educational, motivational, and personal development books, include the titles below:

Wives of the Same School: Tributes and Straight Talk

The Story of Saint Finbarr's College: Contributions to Education and Sports Development in Nigeria

Physics of Soccer II: Science and Strategies for a Better Game

Kitchen Dynamics: The rice way

Consumer Economics: The value of dollars and sense for money management

Youth Soccer Training Slides: A Math and Science Approach

My Little Blue Book of Project Management

8 by 3 Paradigm for Time Management

Badiru's Equation of Student Success: Intelligence, Common Sense, and Self-discipline

Isi Cookbook: Collection of Easy Nigerian Recipes

Blessings of a Father: Education contributions of Father Slattery at Saint Finbarr's College

Physics in the Nigerian Kitchen: The Science, the Art, and the Recipes

The Physics of Soccer: Using Math and Science to Improve Your Game

Getting things done through project management

DEDICATION

This book is dedicated to all wives, who nag and nudge their husbands onto the path of excellence and stand by them no matter what, whenever the husbands fall prey to the failings of man

ACKNOWLEDGMENTS

I acknowledge the immense contributions of my loving my wife of over four decades, Iswat, for nagging me onto the path or righteousness in all I do.

I acknowledge the fun and relevance provided by the syndicated newspaper comics of LOCKHORNS and Blondie. My thanks go to their distributor, King Features Syndicate Inc., for granting me the permission to reprint the comics in this book.

INTRODUCTION

This is a fun cartoon-based book, which is dedicated to showering praises and tributes on wives for their unflinching support, commitment, and personal sacrifice. Both commercial and personal cartoons are used to help communicate the messages in the book. The versatility of wives cannot be overstated. The premise of this book is that women are biologically wired to be care takers of all. Mothers and wives, in particular, are the ultimate care takers. Wives have a natural instinct and disposition to be caring and nurturing. This book is not prejudicial against husbands, but it points out comical and adorable facts about husband-and-wife pairs.

This book takes a humorous look at husband-wife relationships. While there are facts and fictions in the contents, the overall theme and premise of the book is to have fun with everyday observations in marital scenarios and man-and-woman social relationships.

This book is not intended to debase or glorify any gender. It is intended as a comic relief that brings laughter to all readers, which, after all, as medical experts tell us, is essential for good health. Happy and fun reading!

CHAPTER ONE

The Efficacy of Wives

"A wife's job is never done." – Deji Badiru

Wives are from the same school of "How to be a wife." Wives, regardless of where they are located geographically in the world, react similarly to their husbands' actions. No matter how old or young they are, no matter how rich or poor they are, no matter how socially elite they are, no matter their race or creed, no matter their education level, no matter their politics, no matter their religion, and no matter how long they have been married, all wives act the same way toward their husbands. It is as if they have all attended the same school, where they have been instructed in the common characteristics of a wife. The efficacy of wives is multi-dimensional. However, their efficacy has its humorous aspects, and the straight talk you will be treated to here will include a good deal of comic relief. The LOCKHORNS˚ comic below seems to reflect the hilarious nature of marriage. As the front cover suggests, the ladies transition, adorably, from graduation to "wife-dom."

"WIVES ARE GREAT, IF YOU CAN AFFORD ONE."

The testimony offered in this book is based upon my own observations about the efficacy of wives in the society. After more than four decades of marriage, I have observed a lot of behaviors from those on both sides of the matrimonial aisle.

They are from the same school!
"Wives of the Same School" is a book of comical but serious tributes to wives, who are often underappreciated in spite of their multi-faceted contributions. The book borders on offering a marriage-counseling session for husbands. If the book can save a few marriages by changing husbands' perspectives, then it would have done its job!

No husband wants to be controlled by the wife, but control by the wife is exactly what is often needed.

For those not yet married, the contents of the book could be great for advance heads-up. If you know what to expect, you will know how to accept it and cope with it . . . and move on in matrimonial harmony.

Mr. Husband, if you are thinking of changing your wife, for whatever reason, don't bother. They are all from the same school. The next one will be just like the current one.

The stories and presentations are compiled in a comical way to inform and entertain the readers. With copyright permissions, the pages of the book are sprinkled with several reprints of commercial syndicated comic strips spoofing husband-and-wife gaffes. The LOCKHORNS and Blondie are my favorites among the syndicated newspaper comics. The efficacy of wives is that wives call the shots – regardless of what the husband thinks. Some husbands even claim that being told what to do or not do by the wife is viewed as "unmansculating" or taking away the husband's masculinity. But the fact is that being told what to do or not do by the wife is exactly what the husband needs in order to be saved from himself.

Having been married for over four decades and being affiliated with many long-married couples, I have come to a personal observational anecdotal realization that wives think alike, talk alike, and work alike when it comes to taking care of their husbands and the household. Sorry guys, the reverse is not necessarily true, at least not in all cases. It is well known that a wife does not mind putting her own pursuits aside for the sake of her husband's pursuits.

They are from the same school and they know it themselves. Case in point: I was at a neighborhood garage sale recently, where a group of ladies were the vendors. I picked several knick-knacks from around the displays. When I got to cashier, I requested a friendly hefty discount, which the ladies promptly obliged to. One of them commented that I was getting a great deal on the items. I responded by saying, "I will have to wait until I hear my wife's judgement on the purchase of all the unneeded widgets and gadgets." Another lady, obviously a wife, chimed in with some advice. "Just keep them in the garage for a while." Everybody chuckled. Then, she said, "We," referring to themselves, "know these things." So, wives do know. Yes, they are from the same school.

Whether through nature, nurture, or mentor, wives play diverse roles in the home. They serve roles in the examples below:

- Adviser (as in professional challenges)
- Advocate (as in promoting the husband's cause)
- Caretaker (as in family health)
- Chauffeur (as in shuttling the family)
- Cleaner (as in cleaning up after the family)
- Comforter (as in hard times)
- Commander (as in issuing commands to the family)
- Communicator (as in sharing information)
- Confidant (as in being the sounding board of ideas)
- Controller (as in being in control of the family's affairs)
- Cook (as in the kitchen)
- Counselor (as in counseling husband)
- Defender (as in standing up for the family)
- Fighter (as in standing up for husband)
- Friend (as in common pursuits)
- Hardliner (as in asking tough questions)
- Homemaker (as in household economics)
- Instructor (as in instructing the husband on what to do or not do)
- Lover (as in demonstrating acts of love)
- Nagger (as in pointing out errors)
- Organizer (as in decoration)
- Overseer (as in providing adult supervision)
- Protector (as in covering up for husband and protecting the family)
- Re-collector (as in recollecting and remembering everything the husband has forgotten)
- Safer (as in being the money manager) and penny pincher)
- Social connector (as in family representation)
- Softy (as in providing moderation)
- Spender (as in shopping)
- Spokesperson (as in reaching out)
- Stabilizer (as in being the solid rock of the family)
- Stickler for details (as in doctor's office)
- Wardrobe adviser (as in critiquing choice of attire)

- Wealth of wisdom (as in making the right calls)

Wives even serve as disciplinarians, if and when called for. Name it; whatever it is, wives do it all. It is for these various reasons that I have extreme respect and admiration for all wives, indeed, for all women. Thank God there is a wife in the room to provide adult supervision for crucial family endeavors.

Advocacy for Wife's Day

Wives are from the same school. Very much as mothers get recognized with the annual Mother's Day celebration and the acknowledgment that "a mother's work is never done, it is important to recognize equally that a wife's job is never done, as advocated by the opening quote at the beginning of this chapter. Granted that most wives transition to becoming mothers, it is still important to recognize, explicitly, the special roles of a wife in any husband-wife enclave. In this regard, I advocate establishing a "Wives Day" similar to "Mother's Day." Although a "Wife Appreciation Day" is already celebrated informally on the third Sunday in September, through the medium of this book, I am formalizing a "Wives Day" through the formal establishment of www.WivesDay.org, which is now an active website. The website will continue to develop and flourish over the coming years, in alignment with the existing Wife Appreciation Day.

You just have to love wives for their consistency of actions and reactions to their husbands' actions. Not long ago, I was a part of a supervisor training seminar on combatting sexual assault. When certain scenarios were portrayed, a senior manager in the group commented that "if I did any of those acts, my wife would kill me." Everyone laughed. A married lady in the audience then commented, "I will get my hands around his neck and squeeze tightly." Another man in the audience said, "That sounds like my wife." Yes, indeed, it sounds like all wives. If you think you are well off, just wait until your wife gets a hold of your neck, should you be caught with a transgression. A man was once asked if he ever tells white lies. He responded, "Of course, I always tell little white lies to my wife. It is the only way I have lived this long." ☺

"I DID TELL YOU I WAS WELL OFF BEFORE WE WERE MARRIED ... AND I WAS."

Absence of Schadenfreude

They are from the same school. No matter how a wife appears to be maternally oppressive on the husband, there is an inherent absence of schadenfreude on her part. "Schadenfreude" is a German-based word meaning how a person derives pleasure from another person's misfortune. It is a common human flaw recognized by social scientists and psychologists in the study of human relationships. I am convinced that when it comes to issues affecting the husband, there is an absence of schadenfreude in the wife. A wife is inherently committed to avoiding, mitigating, and preempting misfortunes from the affairs of the husband.

CHAPTER TWO

Versatility of Wives

Wives have multi-faceted and multi-dimensional roles in the lives of their husbands. They naturally take on roles whether or not the roles have been conceded to them. Wives have the natural tendencies to take charge of issues for the benefit of their husbands. Many times, wives come across as being overbearing on husbands, but it is all for good. I have harbored the wish to write this book for many years. The eventual motivational drive to do it is the syndicated LOCKHORNS newspaper comic, the contents of which match my own observational experiences with husband-wife relationships. My favorite avocation is to write about everyday events, interpersonal issues, and social observations. The versatility of wives, as communicated through cartoon comics, fits my passion of socially-oriented writing. The theme in this chapter is to present funny representations of the various aspects of a wife's versatile interactions with her husband and his environment. Please read on to enjoy the various accounts "on" the wife's accomplishments, travails, attributes, and characteristics.

Home is Where the Wife is

There is nothing wrong with the popular saying of "Home is where the Heart is." But in the context of this book, my contention is that "home is where the wife is." A wife is the ultimate maker of the home. Without a wife, a place of abode is just a house. With a wife, a man gets a home. As an anniversary present to my wife, my 2007 original line sketch of our then home aptly conveys the role of a wife in the home through my personal quote. Yes, indeed, "home is where the heart is; but the wife is what makes the home." The house in the sketch is our first home built in Beavercreek, Ohio in 2007, after moving from Knoxville, Tennessee in 2006. We have since built another home in the continual tradition of making new homes. In each case, the framed portrait moves with us. Yes, wives are from the same school.

"Home is where the heart is;
Wife is what makes the home"
- Adedeji Bodunde Badiru, September 25, 2007

On Being Healthcare Enforcer

A wife is the enforcer of the home. She makes things happen. She ensures the husband gets his much-needed flu shots and other preventive medical screening. If he refuses or dilly-dally, she enforces the needful, sometimes to the point of almost dragging him to where he needs to be. Many a time, it is the wife who ensures that the husband follows up with medical appointments. She insists to be present whenever the doctor's consultation takes place because she does not trust the husband to accurately or fully recount whatever the doctor's instructions are. For insurance and life risk purposes, actuarial studies do confirm that those who have wives tend to live longer than those who don't. It must be because the wives make sure the husbands get appropriate medical services on a timely schedule.

"MR. 'I-DON'T-NEED-A-FLU-SHOT' IS HERE."

"PLEASE DON'T REFER LEROY FOR A SECOND OPINION...IT WAS HARD ENOUGH GETTING HIM HERE IN THE FIRST PLACE."

On the Cooking Chore

Good cook or not, the wife, in many cases, is still the overseer of the cooking chore at home whether she does it herself, instructs the husband to do it, delegates it to the children, or pays hired help to do it. When she cooks well, she is taken for granted. When she doesn't cook well, she may be mocked. She assumes the responsibility, direct or indirectly, nonetheless.

"WHEN YOU MAKE SOMETHING THAT'S SLOW-COOKED, LORETTA, YOU'RE JUST DELAYING THE INEDIBLE."

On Non-Equality of Husbands

Much has been said and written about men and women being from "different planets" in terms of attributes, characteristics, and interests. In this regard, it is true when we factor in the smarts of each gender. Wives tend to exhibit better judgment, sympathy, empathy, and social considerations in their decision-making processes.

©2012 WM. HOEST ENTERPRISES, INC. Distributed by King Features Syndicate.   www.thelockhorns.com

"MEN AND WOMEN WILL NEVER BE EQUALS UNTIL MEN BECOME SMARTER."

On Who Really Makes Home Decisions

The husband may think he has the primary rights, authority, and entitlement for making family decisions, but the wife makes the ultimate decision for the benefit of everyone in the home. She seizes the opportunity to make the right decision for the family whenever a void is detected. Yes, the real household decisions are made at the wife-level. She is the "management level," where home decisions are made to stick.

"SORRY ... ALL OF MY DECISIONS ARE MADE AT THE WIFE LEVEL."

On Husband's Childlike Acts

Wives are from the same school. A wife is always at work on the husband, for good or bad, for better or for worse. The dedication of a wife is insurmountable, no matter how testy the situation. Call it nature, call it form, call it group think, call it nurture, or what have you, all wives tend to come from the same school of like-minded beings. All wives cater to their husbands just as they cater to their children regarding childlike acts that border on immaturity.... and they are not timid is saying so.

"NO WOMAN WITH A HUSBAND IS CHILDLESS."

On Union Cost of Marriage

"Till death do us part" is the common theme of a marital union. The cost of marriage is a blessing that keeps on giving. A cost-versus-value analysis will confirm a wife's worth in the home. It is a lifelong union sign-up. Continue paying your union dues and you will continue to reap the benefits for the long-term. You will pay now and continue to pay in the future. It is the right of passage for being a husband. So, get with it.

* "I KNEW MARRIAGE WAS A UNION . . . I JUST DIDN'T KNOW ABOUT ALL THESE UNION DUES."

On Critiquing the Husband's Decisions

Whatever the husband's decision is, the wife is sure to judge it, good or bad, mostly always bad. If the husband thinks it is a good decision, the wife will likely think otherwise. It takes courage and determination to not let the criticism crawl all over your nerves. A wife judges the husband's decisions and never fails to offer a critical assessment. Such critiques are often not well received, but always silently appreciated, even in the face of an active pushback. Good decision or bad decision, the husband if still subject to being wrong.

"YOU MARRIED ME AND NOW YOU WANT TO
LECTURE ME ABOUT MAKING BAD DECISIONS?"

"BUT IF I'M ALWAYS WRONG AND I AGREE WITH YOU,
DOESN'T THAT MAKE YOU WRONG?"

On Superior Memory to Remember Stuff

Wives remember all of the items that the husband has long forgotten. Forgetting on the part of the husband may be due to not ascribing a high level of importance to the item. So, it is stored in short-term memory and soon quickly "forgotten." But not so for the wife. All things are important and worthy of remembering for the long term. So, each item is stored in long-term memory by the wife, but for instantaneous recollection whenever needed. Absolutely no statute of limitations in this regard. A wife's Wi-Fi-like memory is the first computer in operation, long before the invention of electronic computers.

"WAKE UP, LEROY! I WANT TO DISCUSS SOMETHING YOU SAID TO ME FIFTEEN YEARS AGO."

"I SAID THAT TWELVE YEARS AGO...ISN'T THERE A STATUTE OF LIMITATIONS?"

On Advising the Husband

Whether needed or not, whether solicited or not, the wife's advice is always available. There is no point resisting the offer of advice. Even if you ignore it, it will keep on coming, unabated. The wife is like the in-house, onsite consultant for critical decision-making. She sees it as her marital right and entitlement. You should just comply or feign compliance, just to maintain peace.

There is the joke about the husband who claims he does not need a GPS (Global Positioning System) while driving because his side-by-side wife offers natural directional guidance. The wife is really the first edition of "Siri" and "Alexa." The only difference is that the husband can ignore instructions from Siri, but dare not ignore those from the wife. If he does, he does so at his own peril.

"OF COURSE I DON'T MIND YOU GIVING ME ADVICE...
AS LONG AS YOU DON'T MIND MY IGNORING IT."

On Playing Hookie

In the comic below, Leroy claims that he gets his leisure time by hiding from his wife. Playing hookie never works on either side. On the flip side, a joke goes as follows. A man and his wife go shopping in a department store. The wife disappears among the aisles in search of bargains in the nooks and corners of the store, one after the other. The husband, after waiting for several minutes without being able to find the wife comes up with a wife-finding ploy. He approaches a sexy beautiful lady and says, "Excuse me, I can't find my wife, can I talk to you?" The sexy lady says "Okay, I don't mind, but how is that going to help you find your wife?" He replies, "Trust me, as soon as I start talking to you, my wife will appear out of nowhere."

"MY LEISURE TIME IS WHEN MY WIFE CAN'T FIND ME."

In a similar vein of playing hookie or hide-and-seek with the wife, a joke goes as follows:

A suspicious wife calls her husband on his cell phone.
Wife: Where are you, Bob?
Bob: At home, my love.
Wife: Are you sure?
Bob: Yes.
Wife: Okay, Turn on the blender in the kitchen.
Bob: Blend, blend, blend goes the sound of the blender.
Wife: Ok, Bob, talk to you later.

Another day arrives:
Still suspicious, the Wife calls: Where are you now, Bob?
Bob: At home love.
Wife: Are you sure?
Bob: Yes.
Wife: Turn on the blender.
Bob: Blend, blend, blend goes the noise of the blender.

Wife: Okay, bye for now.

The next day, the wife decides to go home earlier than expected. She finds her son alone in the house.
"Joe, where is your father?"
Son: "I don't know, he went out carrying the blender with him."

The moral of the joke: That's for the reader to decipher.

On Husband's Selective Listening

The husband hears what and when he wants to hear. "Honey, honey, where are you/" Dead silence is often the answer to this common wifely call. With selective hearing, the husband can even listen without actually hearing the wife. There is an unsubstantiated story of a husband who feigned being deaf and dumb for decades, just to avoid listening to his wife. That is an arrant display of stupidity and insensitivity. The wife of a colleague once called me on the phone, "Where is Bob? I have been calling him on his cell phone and he is not picking up. He should have been home by now. Would you happen to know where he is?" Of course, I did not know. I replied, "He is probably busy, I will check on him and let you know." I called Bob and he answered right away. "Ann has been calling you without answer. She is worried. She just called me to inquire. She thought your boss might know your whereabouts. You better call her to keep her mind at ease." Bob chuckled, "Oh, she gets antsy when she can't reach me quickly, but it is usually for something not important or urgent." Bob is wrong. To the wife, every reason to call is urgent and important. It doesn't matter whether you are busy at work or in a high-level meeting, the wife must be able to reach you. When the wife calls, it is an emergency, whether it, actually, is or not. You can't avoid the wifely sermon by not answering your phone call. Sooner or later, you gonna get it!

"I'M HERE BECAUSE I'D RATHER HEAR YOUR SERMON THAN MY WIFE'S."

On Wives as Teleprompters

All jokes aside, if not for wives, many men would never learn their lessons. Wives have a knack for being able to signal their husbands on what to say or not say in a social setting. This is often most evident when they disapprove of the husbands' carefree utterances. They would use signals of winking, head scratching, ear pulling, legs taps, and kicks under the table to right their husbands' wrongs. A husband dare not ignore these subtle signals. There was a classic 2019 case of the Governor of Virginia, who found himself in a political turmoil and was about to stick his foot deeper into his mouth, so to speak, until his wife, standing beside him, instructed him that "then and there" was not the appropriate forum for further talk. He obliged and saved himself from further embarrassment and, subsequently, saved his job. As Mrs. Lockhorns might opine, things that are better left unsaid are the things husbands say.

"THE THINGS BETTER LEFT UNSAID ARE THE THINGS LEROY SAYS."

A colleague once advised, "when dealing with the wife, just keep your mouth shut; for anything you say, good or bad, will be held against you."

The common saying goes as "Silence is the best answer for a fool."
In my book, there is a twist to the common saying and it goes as "Silence is the best answer of a husband when he is wrong."

Learn to hold your tongue and your frown because sentiments expressed or implied can ruin a spousal relationship, even in cases where your opinion has been explicitly requested. This happens often when the wife asks a question such as "honey, how does this dress look on me?"

To celebrate the efficacy of long-married couples, I wrote the following fictional account for comic relief:

==========================

Mental Images: Why Some Married Couples Look Alike

On a recent reflective afternoon, my thoughts wandered to a comment that our longtime friends often make about my wife and me. "You two really look alike!" I have heard this so many times that I was beginning to believe it. Maybe, I really want to believe it. You see, my wife really looks much better than I do. So, it is gratifying to be likened to such a beautiful person. Jokes aside, I questioned whether there was, indeed, a rational explanation for couples, who have been married a long time, to actually look alike.

I rummaged through my mind, both the scientific and the naive. Nothing came to the surface immediately. I reasoned, maybe some married couples look alike because they are actually related through some distant family tree. I struggled to mentally trace my family tree to search for remote possibilities of where my family tree and my wife's family tree could have crossed in the distant past. I drew a blank. Maybe our friends lie about us looking alike just to express the common social compliment that is supposed to make everyone feel good.

After several minutes of mental digression, I was jolted back to the reality of the task at hand, grading test papers. For several days thereafter, the thoughts of married couples, who look alike, tried to creep back into my mind. But I consciously fought the thought because I knew that no matter how hard I might meditate, I would not be able to explain this perplexing mystery; and I was not about to spend several valuable minutes battling an impossible puzzle. It was a tug-of-war. The puzzle tried to come back, I resisted. Sometimes, I deliberately teased the puzzle, bringing myself to the brink of serious contemplation, only to back out at the last instant because I knew I could not successfully engage the puzzle.

Then, one dreary rainy morning, Eureka! Without even trying hard, I realized that what we think we see is not usually what we actually see. What we think we see is a matter of what our brains interpret as the signals coming from our eyes. Bingo, I have inadvertently solved the puzzle of why long-married couples look alike.

The reason is that those who see the couple as looking alike are those who are accustomed to seeing the couple together. Thus, when you see one spouse, the mental image about the visage of the other spouse subconsciously comes to the surface, and you may actually think that you are seeing the other spouse. In other words, the image of the other spouse is superimposed on the image of the present spouse. This explains why the comment is made, most frequently, by those who have known the couple for a long time. New acquaintances are more likely to reach the valid conclusion that the spouses do not look alike at all.

======================

The Value of "Naggermosity"

They are from the same school! All wives are very "naggermous" (my own term) and magnanimous toward their husbands, from a loving perspective. Fortunately, in my own case, all that nagging has done me a world of good over the past several decades! Marriages often start to crumble when the man can no longer take all the nagging. My bottom-line advice to men is to take the nagging in stride and move forward with what the wife wants. The husband will never win a nagging contest against the wife. So, why bother. Take it and preserve your good relationship. My goal is to use the medium of "Wives of the Same School" to pay tribute to wives while being frank and humorous about the man-woman differences. If any reader finds the direct references too direct and close to home, I apologize in advance. The bottom line is that the "Mag-naggermous" wife, who is a magnanimous wife to her husband is also the mag-nagger-most wife.

"HOW CAN THEY CALL THIS REALITY?
I HAVEN'T HEARD ANY NAGGING YET."

Wives are biologically wired to be care takers. Based on the hypothesis of this book, wives belong to the same school of similar characteristics, granted that there are some modern exceptions. Key indicators and confirmation can be seen and or heard in various testimonials. Let us consider the following quotes of confirmations:

"We always hold hands. If I let go, she shops." - Henry Youngman, Comedian

"That's the odd thing about wives. It's the only person in the world you know can't beat you in a fight, but you're still scarred of them more than anybody else." - Comedian Chris Rock

"Men with pierced ears are better prepared for marriage; they've experienced pain and bought jewelry." – Comic Rita Rudner

A wife texts her husband on a frosty Winter morning. "Windows frozen"

Her husband texts back, "Pour lukewarm water over it."

A few minutes later comes her reply, "Computer is completely messed up now." – Catherin Hiscox, Hemel Hempstead, Great Britain (from Reader's Digest, January 2013, p. 13)

You cannot out-scream a wife; so why bother?

The husband goes into a store and within 5 minutes he generates $200 worth of economic impact. By comparison, the wife goes into a store, spends three hours and comes out with only $5 worth of economic impact.

Wives complain that husbands take the fun out of shopping. They just go into a store and come out without experiencing the full vibes of the store. Wives, on the other hand, take their time to enjoy the sights and sounds of shopping.

On Non-Speaking Terms

An interesting gag about a couple not on speaking terms.
Husband left a note on the wife's bedroom dresser: "Please wake me up at 6am so that I won't miss my important job interview."

At 6am the next morning, the wife left a written note on the husband's side of the bed in response: "Michael, it is 6am, please wake up so that you won't miss your job interview."

To Split or Not to Split

The common slang for divorce is split. Gossip columns in the popular press often highlight the juicy talks of who is splitting from whom and what is available to split between the splitting couple. My original caricature below conveys that what binds a couple together may be the adversity of the relationship. In the modern divorce court, splitting of matrimonial assets can become contentious. Is there anything to split in a divorce settlement? Who owns what? Who is entitled to what? How should assets be split? If there is nothing to split, maybe it is not worth splitting at all.

On Resolution of Arguments

They are from the same school. Now, you know. But, did you know that long-married couples bicker the most? The wife is always right in such squabbles. So, why bother to argue. Since you cannot out-argue the wife, why enter into an argument at all? Peace will reign supreme in the household if you elect not to argue with the wife.

**"I'D LIKE TO AGREE WITH YOU, LEROY, BUT THEN
WE'D BOTH BE WRONG."**

Giving Orders

The wife is the Sergeant-at-Arms in the house. It is her official household to oversee, direct, and manage. Her duty includes maintaining order, safety, and security in the home. Her sense of duty is to ensure that the husband complies, whether or not he understands. This leads to the following military-service joke:

Q: Why do women like marrying service men?
A: Because they are already used to taking orders

**"YOU'RE NOT SUPPOSED TO UNDERSTAND ME . . .
YOU'RE SUPPOSED TO DO AS I SAY."**

Shopping Differences and Preferences

Although these testimonials are written in the first-person tense for ease of story reporting, the actual names of the perpetrators and victims are masked to protect both the innocent and the guilty.

Wives often accuse their husbands of taking the fun out of shopping. They just want to rush into the store and rush out, purchasing only one thing or nothing at all. They fail to enjoy the sights and sounds of store cruising. When a married couple shops together, you can always guess how long the couple has been married. The long-married couples tend to argue more in store aisles about what and what is being looked at and considered for purchase. Newly-married couples argue less because they are still in the concession stage of give-and-take. Once they cross into the marital familiarity region, they argue more about relative shopping preferences. The essay that follows presents another interesting conjecture about long-married couples.

It is a nice Saturday afternoon. My wife, apparently getting bored, asks me if I would accompany her on a quick run to the friendly neighborhood shopping mall. It is friendly because she seems to spend a lot of time there. Well, I don't see any harm if it is going to be quick, even though I know deep down that no wife's trip to the mall, or any store for that matter, is ever quick. Anyway, I say yes. That is my first mistake. Anyway, we are at the mall and we make a stop at every storefront, for what appears to be an endless duration. I am sure we are not actually intending to buy anything, but it sure seems that we are seriously looking for something important, the urgent purchase of which has an implication for the family's total welfare. Noting the protracted urgency, or lack thereof, I slowly migrate from my wife's side, I walk into the center aisle and proceed to stroll down leisurely at a pace that I am sure she will be able to catch up with me whenever she decides to make an exit from a store. Each store's magnetic forces seem to grow stronger the more time we spend in the store. This type of aimless drifting of accompanying husbands is the reason many shopping malls now have a husband-sitting service area. Wherever a babysitter service may be needed, a husband-sitter service equally makes sense.

As I am making my way through the center aisle, I occasionally look back to ensure I am not too many paces beyond my wife's beckoning call of "Honey, did you see that? They want $20 bucks for that. I can get it for 15 at Walmart." I never come into the store, how can she expect me to see "that"? For each call, I glance back and say, "oh yes, I see it. They must be out of their mind asking for such a ridiculous price." This response always makes her happy, as it confirms that I am paying attention to whatever she is doing, or not doing. It also confirms to her that I am on her side in the price-assessing war. Even though she ought to know that those responses are concocted and not the absolute truth, she always accepts them. That is good enough for our togetherness.

Well, on this particular afternoon, as I drift down the center aisle, the whole world must be noticing that I am deliberately trying to disengage from my wife's shop-to-shop excursion. The proof of this is what happens next.

An elderly lady, who, I am sure, is also being evaded by her co-shopper husband, walks up beside me and mutters directly in my face, as if chastising me,

"You men take the fun out of shopping."

I, of course, don't respond. I just look at her inquisitively, asking in my mind, "Excuse me."

I do not want to start an argument with a bevy of like-minded schoolmates. That is, the wives from the same school.

The converse of the shopping testimony is the case where the couple goes to a hardware store instead to a regular department store. Husbands are within their elements when they shop for hardware items while most wives are abhorrent to buying more hardware toys. My own favorite spots are at Lowe's, Home Depot, ACE Hardware store, and other similarly-stocked shops. I can disappear into the aisles of hardware for hours. Weekend morning are great for watching men walk aimlessly, but with excited eyes, around the aisles of hardware stores.

Many times, I pray fervently before going into a hardware store. "God, let me not find something to buy that I don't need to buy today." Even if I already have duplicates of the same item, it may still be manly satisfying to buy an additional copy for parallel redundancy backup purposes. A wife's passion for purchasing shoes and handbags are akin to the husband's passion for acquiring more hardware gadgets.

On Incessant Talking

Wives are blessed with a remarkable endurance of lung compression for uttering sound and composing talk. No matter how much and how long a wife has talked all day, she is still ready and willing to talk some more. It is a surprise to me that more wives are not in the legal profession, where prolonged arguments, testimony, and cross-examination are the norm. In fact, wiki reports in 2013 that only 40% of practicing lawyers is made up of women. It ought to be far more than that.

Reference: http://wiki.answers.com/Q/
What percentage of lawyers are women

"IF YOU'D STOP TALKING, I'D LISTEN."

"I BOUGHT THIS HOPING WE CAN TALK MORE
IF WE STAND AROUND IT."

On Going Out Together

One sunny Saturday, I inform my wife that I need to visit the local post office to mail a package. She responds, "I'll go with you so that I can stop by the shoe repair store. I know I have just invited trouble. Based on past experience, I know one shoe store will migrate into multiple shoe stores or something else of the shopping caliber. The plan is to first go to the Post Office, so that I can have my mission accomplished, then proceed on to the shoe store. Well, we set out heading to the post office. Half way down, she spots a yard sale sign and begs for us to stop, "just to look." I insist we go to the post office first, otherwise, by the time we are done "just looking," the Post Office will have closed for the day. Fortunately, she agrees. After the post office, she reminds me of the yard sale. "What about the shoe store?" We will go there after the yard sale. Okay.

We stop at the yard sale, where she proceeds to just look at everything on display for a great bargain. Reminding her that the shoe store might close early on a Saturday, hoping that will encourage her to leave the yard cruising alone. It does not work. So, I resort to my familiar mall-aisle strolling away from the main stage. When she finally finds a piece of "furniture" she has been "wanting for years," she decides to buy it. Betraying her complete disregard of geometry, she calls me to come over to help load the furniture onto our SUV, the internal volume of which is not sufficient to haul the behemoth item she just bought. She worries only about the algebra of the savings emanating from the good price. The geometry of hauling the huge purchase home does not matter. I tried to convince her of the geometrical incompatibility, but she will have none of it, saying, "just try it. At this point, one of the husbands came over to me and whispered. Don't worry, I get that too. I immediately felt better. After all, I am not the only husband treated this way. There is a brotherhood of the "spousally-oppressed" husbands as confirmed by the following words that wives use to describe their errant husbands:

- Stubborn
- Inattentive
- Insensitive
- Unfocused
- Uncommunicative
- Distracted
- Childish
- Over-dependent

On the Power of Gossip

Should we say "the power of communication?" Gossip is nothing more than an effective way of communication, whatever the subject of the communication might be. Wives are the ultimate communicators. One parody says there are many ways to spread communication (aka, rumor, gossip), including the following:

- Telephone
- Television
- Telegraph
- "Tell-a-woman" (Apologies, this is just a parody actually fueled by a woman)

We often need to listen to rumors and gossips (carefully) because sometimes there may be snippets of useful facts that could not be obtained through other means.

"I DO NOT REPEAT GOSSIP... THAT'S WHY PEOPLE HAVE TO LISTEN CAREFULLY THE FIRST TIME."

On the Need for More Storage Space

Because of their overall management of household affairs, wives always need more space. The additional space that a wife seeks may not always be for her own use alone. Sometimes, the wife stores items of general household needs within her own space for safekeeping and property protection. Many times, the wife takes custody of family items she is not sure would be safe within the husband's storage space. So, please give space credit where and when it is due.

"WHEN A WIFE SAYS SHE NEEDS MORE SPACE,
SHE MEANS MORE OF YOURS."

"YOU CAN'T RETIRE, LEROY ... THIS HOUSE ISN'T
BIG ENOUGH FOR THE TWO OF US."

On Controlling Household Projects

They are from the same school. Many times, it appears that wives are full of extreme negativity and criticism about their husbands' actions. But it is all for the long-term benefit of the entire family.

The wives are, by default, always in the construction business around the home, mostly by supervising the do-it-yourself (DIY) projects by their husbands. If it is not approved by the wife, it may not be done. If it is approved and not done well, all the household will hear about it. The decision-making, critiquing, and censuring mentioned earlier all come down to bear on the assessment of the husband's project execution accomplishments. The LOCKHORNS typify this realization perfectly through their comics.

"LORETTA SAY NO TO A MAN CAVE?"

"OF COURSE THE WARRANTY EXPIRED ... IT TOOK YOU TWO YEARS TO PUT IT TOGETHER."

"WELL, NOW WE KNOW HOW WE'LL SPEND THE $350 YOU SAVED BY DOING IT YOURSELF."

THE LOCKHORNS BY BUNNY HOEST

"I'VE TOLD YOU BEFORE, LEROY ... IF YOU WANT SOMETHING DONE RIGHT, LET SOMEONE ELSE DO IT!"

"I AM **NOT** BEING CRITICAL ... I'M JUST POINTING OUT EVERYTHING YOU'RE DOING WRONG."

CHAPTER THREE

Husband-and-Wife Jokes

This chapter presents a collection of jokes that I have heard over the years. Many have been rewritten or adapted from other jokes so that they will apply to our contemporary context.

==================

A husband would pay $2 for a $1 item he needs.
A woman will pay $1 for a $2 item that she doesn't need but it's on sale.

==================

On New Year's Eve, Daniel was in no shape to drive, so he sensibly left his car in the bar's parking lot and walked home. As he was wobbling along, he was stopped by a policeman.

'What are you doing out here at four o'clock in the morning?' asked the police officer.

'I'm on my way to a lecture,' answered Daniel.

'And who on earth, in his or her right mind, is going to give a lecture at this time on New Year's Eve?' inquired the police officer sarcastically.

'My wife,' slurred Daniel grimly.

==================

The comical cliché works for all wives.

"A man in the house is worth two in the street." - **Mae West**

The sage, Mae West, has been confirmed to know a thing or two about man-woman relationships. Who are we to dispute this assertion?

==================

"Men, don't criticize your wife's poor choices; you are one of them." - Source unknown

==================

It is true that the husband is the Head of the family. But the wife is the Neck of the family; and the neck can pretty well turn the head whichever way she wants.

Thank God for wives; Or a lot of men would have their feet permanently stuck in their mouths . . . . saying the wrong things at the wrong times.

==================

Quotable quote:

"If you want something said, ask a man; if you want something done, ask a woman."
    - **Margaret Thatcher**

The quote above is a cogent testimony to the common belief that "women are wired to multitask and succeed at it."

"Success of a marriage cannot always be traced to the presence of communication, but failure can be traced to its absence."

==================

In spite of all these discordant examples, the fact is that true love does exist between the husband and the wife, as surmised by Shakespeare below:

"The course of true love never did run smooth." - Shakespeare

==================

Comic by the author:

Couple in front of a divorce judge . . .
Judge: Why are you doing this?
Husband: Irreconcilable differences!
Judge: Well, Ma'am, what's your response?
Wife: I object! We can't afford to split because we have nothing to split.

==================

"Showbiz people tell you just what you want to hear. But my wife tells me the truth, almost to a fault." - Ray Romano

Ray also went on to call his wife a saint, "a saint who curses," at him, "but still a saint." Yes, I agree with Ray. A wife is the only one who will be brutally truthful in telling a husband what a *stupid* idea he has. While others are falsely oooing and aahing about a man's brilliant ways, it is only his wife who will frankly advise him that he ain't so.

==================

A wife called her husband on his cell phone.
Wife: "Honey where are you?"
Husband: "I'm at the bank."
Wife: "Dear, please I need $200 to activate my blackberry, $150 to do my hair, and $250 to buy a dress."
Husband: "sorry, Sweetie, I am at the bank of a river. Do you want some fish to cook?"

==================

Police Officer: "Sir, you just hit the lamp post. What happened?"
Man Driver: "I was showing my wife how to drive when I accidentally ran into the post."
Officer: Well, sir, this is not how to drive."

==================

Question: What month of the year, in general, do people talk the least?

Answer: The month is February. That is when women are short-changed by two days of the month from talking. But don't worry, they get one of the two days back every four years!

Women are often accused of being yentas (i.e., a woman who is a gossip or busybody). But this perception is not necessarily due to being mischievous. It is often due to the fact that women are endowed with more endurance in the talking game and spreading useful information. Meanwhile, men have neither the "talk" nor "listen-well" attributes.

==================

Wife says to the family doctor: "My husband has this bad habit of speaking while sleeping. What shall I do to stop this?

Family doctor replies: "Have you tried giving him a chance to speak when he is awake?"

==================

Overheard in a family doctor's office:
Husband to wife: "Dear, will you, PLEASE, let the doctor give me the instructions himself."

==================

Joke:
The Japanese have invented a new camera with a shutter so fast that it can catch a woman with her mouth shut.

==================

Based on statistical evidence, social scientists have confirmed that, on the average, married men live longer than unmarried men and women generally live longer than men.

A man's perspective:
Question: Why do women live longer and better than men?

Answer: Very simple, . . . they don't have wives.

Facts and reality:
Men live more self-imposed dangerous lives, such as initiating wars.

==================

"If all the leaders of the world were women, they would spend more time talking and less time fighting."

==================

Scenario: Telephone rings at night
Husband: "If it's for me, please say I'm not at home."
Wife: Answering the phone, "He is at home..."
Husband: Shocked, "What the hell..?"

Wife: Reassuring the husband, "It was for me..."

==================

Doctor: "Has there been any insanity in your family?"
Patient: "Yes, doctor. My husband thinks he's the boss."

==================

Police: "Why did you use a chair to hit your husband?"
Accused: "Because I could not lift the table."

==================

Test question posed to a nurse in training: Name two common male diseases
Answer: Malevolent and Maleficent

FOR SALE BY OWNER.
Complete set of Encyclopedia Britannica, 45 volumes.
Excellent condition - $200 or best offer.
No longer needed – Got married…. Wife knows everything.

==================

A 2012 study revealed that wives are happier when their husbands are miserable.

Why? Because women are designed to be happier when they have somebody to take care of . . . even if they caused that person's agony in the first place.

Conclusion: Women nag more just to get their husbands into a miserable state so that they can then "mother" them.

Readers should note that this conclusion is opposite my theory of the absence of schadenfreude in the wife. Please see an earlier section on this topic.

==================

When a wife says to her husband, "I will kill you," don't believe a word of it. Most wives don't stoop that low.

==================

If a wife asks you, "How do I look?"
Reply as, "You look young to me . . ."

Tips for Husbands

- The secret of wives is their vocal power. No man can compete in that realm.
- On the topic of age, even if you and your wife have been together for ages, you should never call her "old faithful."
- Realize that men only know how to make the money, it is the wives who know how to manage it.

School of Wives

They are from the same school. Wives have diverse characteristics in common, from being deferential, submissive, obedient, compliant, acquiescent, docile, passive, and meek even while being assertive. One thing certain about wives is that they are all of the same school – the same school of thought, the same school of sentiments, the same school of caring, and the same school of husband nagging. Whenever nagging comes, the husband must exhibit super absorbent skin to sit there and take it all. The best strategy for a husband is to keep his mouth shut when spoken to. The secret is out! The common hush-hush story shared in men's circles is that "the wife is always right," but husbands rarely admit that publicly.

First and foremost, wives are mothers too. That basic instinct makes them to stand by their children and husbands when no one else would hang around. Only a mother would not think twice about closely hugging her child even when the child has been confirmed to have a highly contagious disease. A wife, with motherly instinct, would not think twice about standing by her husband in all and every situation. Wives, as mothers, are wonderful. They always exhibit unconditional and unpretentious love for their sons and husbands.

Another common perception is that the wife controls the husband. But the actual fact is that the wife "mothers" the husband, such that the husband is always in good hands — of "parental" control.

Husband-and-wife relationships offer avenues for amusement and wonderment. In the final analysis, the wife is the boss of the house even if she appears to be subserviently cooperating with the husband.

You may be the emperor of your work domain or professional circles, but when you get home, you are liable to being chewed out by the wife for simple acts of commission or omission.

Wives take pleasure in erroneously accusing their husbands of being inattentive, hard of hearing, stubborn, insensitive, household mess maker, not cost conscious, kitchen slobs, and what have you . . . as long as they are the ones making the accusations. They readily pounce on anyone who dares offer the same assessment of their husbands that they themselves volunteer. I have heard wives giggling happily as they share stories of their husbands' respective scalawag ways.

To be fair, some of the wives' accusations are justified. Case in point. Many times, the value of a wife can be measured in dollars saved. After over four decades of marriage, I finally started listening to my wife about checking my cash change at the cashier's counter at grocery stores and department stores. I used to argue that standing there counting change amounted to a waste of everyone's time. After all, we can trust the stores. It is supposed to be a honor system. Well, I was wrong. Within six months of mustering manly courage to stand and count to verify my change, I had saved over $35. Stores do, indeed, commit change errors . . . . either inadvertently or as deliberate business practice (or er eh, business fraud, if we want to be blunt about it). In one case, the cashier gave me a change that is short by $10. I was about to stuff the rumpled up bills into my pocket when I realized I must exercise my verification chores. Lo and behold, I discovered that I was shortchanged. I promptly protested. The cashier did not argue. She calmly called the supervisor and announced "I shorted this guy by $10." The supervisor, equally calmly, did whatever check-out supervisors do when they insert and turn their override cash register key. I got my $10 back. I wish my wife had been there to watch my prudence. She would have been proud of me. Only when she saw it herself would she believe that I was a reformed shopper.

Nagging Sometimes Pays

In spite of the push backs about spousal nagging from wives, it is true that nagging does pay. There is the February 19, 2010 story of an Indiana man who checked his $2.5million winning lottery ticket only after his wife nagged him into action … three days before the ticket expired.

Only your wife will tell you the truth (about your flaws), the whole truth; and nothing but the truth, even if it hurts.

Having a heated argument with your spouse, which is common in marital spats, is as dangerous as driving and texting. For the husband to get in any winning word requires total redirection of mental acuity, which leads to a distraction, which impedes concentration on driving.

Add spousal nagging to the list of driving distractions, along with cell phones, texting, reading, writing, eating, applying makeup, bird watching, and crying babies.

"Wife or Death" Dilemma

The Diet Cop: In the August/September 2012 issue of AARP Magazine, a husband asked the advice columnist, "I was recently diagnosed with high cholesterol. Ever since, my wife has been obsessing about my food intake. I know she's worried about me, but living with a diet cop is making me miserable. **How can I get her to relax?**"

The gist of the advice that came back is something like "Listen to your wife. Your heart, and your wife, will be happier – and so will you." So, do you want death or do you want your wife. Wives have been known to prevent the death of their husbands through their meticulous nagging about healthy eating habits. The questioner gets no sympathy from this author because all husbands go through the same dilemma.

The Lord of the House: It is either that the wives really lord it over their husbands or the husbands inflate the truth when reporting the incident to their colleagues.

Around the work place, it is customary to hear a husband lament their spousal oppression by announcing that "Sue did xyz to me" or "Deb said so so and so to me about my eating habits." If the facts are exaggerated, then the husbands are sarcastically seeking co-worker sympathy or commiseration.

Women are put on this Earth to supervise and control men. Imagine a world without women. Assuming that there are other means of procreation of the male species, men would be a bunch of out-of-control warriors. Their self-destructive ways would effectively impede propagation of the species. Nature knows its boundaries. So, the female was created to serve as a moderating force over the male. Some fun facts:

- When it comes to domestic affairs, the wife is always right.
- The wife controls the TV remote, even if the husband gets it temporarily for the sports channel.
- The wife must give an okay before something in the house can be done.

As we enjoy the comically side of the contents of this book, we should also recognize the social-responsibility of being sensitive to the challenges many families (husbands and wives) face on a daily basis.

Husband's Defender or Nemesis

There is a Nigerian saying that "the mother who invites a disciplinarian into her child's case does not really mean it." Similarly, a wife who makes a comment about her husband's failings will not tolerate other people making the same comment.

Wives are the ultimate defenders of their husbands. Even if a couple is fighting like cats and dogs and the wife bad-mouths the husband publicly, outsiders dare not jump on the bandwagon, because the wife will turn on the outsider. Wives prefer criticizing their husbands themselves, but do not want someone else picking on the husband.

With over two decades of being an administrator, I have learned to judge how men who reported to me feel about by administration by assessing how their wives react to me. While the men might hide their feelings and pretend that things are okay in an attempt to avoid administrative confrontation, their wives definitely don't hide their feelings.

If we are at a social event and the wife of a subordinate warms up to me, then I know her husband must have been telling her good things about me. If, on the other hand, the wife gives me a cold shoulder, then I know I am in trouble with the husband. The wife is on the prowl of seeking redemption.

Don't pick on a husband in the presence of his wife. She might be the one to come after you. Even meek-mannered wives can turn into pit bulls when someone picks on their husbands. With an aggressive-mannered wife, you better watch out. The 2012 Super Bowl case of quarterback Tom Brady's wife, Gisele, is a good case in point. After the 2012 Super Bowl (Super Bowl XLVI) and the heckling of several Giants fans, Gisele was caught on video saying "My husband cannot f_____ throw the ball and catch the ball at the same time!" in defense of her husband. Yes, that is the spirit of a wife, any wife. They are all from the same school.

Wives from the same school of nature

You could raise a woman completely out of contact with any other human being. But the minute she gets married, she'll start behaving the same way as all the other wives from the same school. Same school of nature, that is. Wives take joy in ribbing their own husband, but will not tolerate someone else doing it.

Followership, Leadership, and Teamwork

Who is the real boss in the home? Apart from making decisions, the wife exercises boss-level leadership authority over decisions in the home, but at the same time demonstrates followership and teamwork characteristics.

I cannot count how many times my wife has subconsciously (mind you, not blindly) followed me into the Men's Room of Rest Stops on many of our long road trips. She does this not because of her sense of blind followership; but from the innate sense of teamwork, support, "disciple-ness," or togetherness. I have had to snap "why are you following me here" on various occasions before she would get jolted back to the realization of what she was doing. Wives tend to want to follow even when they are leading. This is not necessarily due to a subservient nature, it is just their way of being compliant with family values and togetherness.

I am a dedicated road observer. On road trips, I have also noticed how couples drive in tandem on the highway when moving in two vehicles. I always get fascinated by observing a particular sequence again and again. Almost always, the husband drives the U-Haul Truck in front; diligently followed by the wife driving the family car. Even when the husband has to signal or call the wife for directions to where they are going, she still lets him lead the way. One interesting observation is that when the wife drives behind, she follows the husband's vehicle very closely. If he slows down, she slows down; never passing him. If he speeds up, she speeds up to stay close; tailgating almost to the point of rear-ending. It is virtually like wanting to keep an eye on him from the rear. On rare occasions that the wife might find herself driving in front, she constantly checks to ensure that she is not out-pacing the husband's vehicle. By contrast, when he drives in front, he sets his speed to suit him, without regard to how close or far behind the wife's vehicle is traveling.

Another observation of wonderment is how, by default, the husband is the one who often drives when husband and wife travel together. This wonderment must have prompted one of my sons, at the age of four, to ask "Daddy, are you the boss of mommy?" I inquired why he raised such a question. He innocently replied, ". . . because you are always driving when we go out with mommy." I took the opportunity to explain to him that driving doesn't necessarily correlate with being the boss. In fact, the person who is driving is most often the subordinate. I comforted my son, the inquirer, that I was really mommy's chauffeur. I said being the driver actually means I drive to wherever mommy wants me to drive to. To which he replied, "That is very nice of you." Kids do, indeed, see things from amusing perspectives.

Wives as smoke signals

You can tell how you are doing at work by how the boss' wife reacts to you in an office social gathering. If the wife warms up to you, you know that the boss has been saying good things about you at home — your work performance, your attitude, your supportive disposition, your attitude, etc. But if the wife ignores you and does not readily acknowledge your presence, that is a smoke signal that the boss has been reporting you negatively to his wife at home. Even the USA First Lady can show displeasure at the president's political detractors, as evidenced by the widely reported rolling of the eyes by Michelle Obama at Speaker John Boehner at a 2013 post-inaugural address luncheon, all because he allegedly said something unappreciated to the president.

Seeking comfort and sympathy at home, male bosses always tell their wives about the scuttle bags they are dealing with at work. Seeing themselves as their husbands redeemers, the wives would always react to the offenders negatively. This does not happen in the case of female bosses. Even though the female boss might tell her husband about work-place scuttle bags, he never displays any emotion one way or the other when he comes in contact with the offending scuttle bags.

"THEY TELL US WE'RE LIKE A FAMILY HERE, BUT WE'RE REALLY MORE LIKE IN-LAWS."

Man Cave is no Refuge

A man cave is supposed to be a refuge of the husband; but it doesn't always work. There is often an invasion by the wife. Whenever the wife bursts in, the husband has to be accommodating to avoid a close-quarter war. They are from the same school.

Even wives who have had no medical training tend to diagnose the ailments of their husbands. Some of the common ailments they accuse their husbands of having include the following:

    1.   not hearing well

2. not listening
3. not caring
4. not seeing too well

==================

Spousal Trade-offs

Every spousal engagement is a project alright; and every project must be managed strategically. Good spouses find themselves. One finds the other and is accepted by the other through the acts of trade-offs and compromise. Finding the perfect match is often an impossible challenge that we should not allow to derail our eventual goals.

Like Pope John Paul II said, marriage unites spouses into a "domestic church." The Church must be managed, nurtured, and glorified. The corporate tools and techniques of project management are essential in accomplishing that goal.

Spats occur in any relationship. The bigger challenge is to keep them from mushrooming into cankerous domestic plaques.

William Shakespeare speaks of "This canker that eats up Love's tender spring" (Venus and Adonis, William Shakespeare, April 18, 1593). Spring brings the aura of love. If not protected in spousal relationships, it can be eaten up by the canker of petty spats.

Some wise person said the following at some time:

Work as if you have no need of the money.
Love as if you've never been hurt.
Dance as if nobody is watching.
Sing as if nobody is listening.
Live as if your spouse were your world.

CHAPTER FOUR

Husband-and-Wife Quotes

The sagacious sayings of sages can help us see the lighter side of husband-wife relationships. This chapter presents additional quotes demonstrating the adorable roles of wives, just for laughs.

"A wife's sense is as sharp as a shadow's edge." – **Deji Badiru**

"Harm can come from the harmless. The most innocuous comment in a spousal relationship may be the most treacherous." – **Deji Badiru**

"I first learned the concept of non-violence in my marriage." – **Gandhi**

"You come to love not by finding the perfect person, but by seeing an imperfect person perfectly." – **Sam Keen**

"A successful marriage requires falling in love many times, always with the same person." – **Mignon McLoughlin**

"My husband and I have never considered divorce… murder sometimes, but never divorce." – **Joyce Brothers**

"The most important thing a father can do for his children is to love their mother." – **Theodore Hesburgh**

"Chains do not hold a marriage together. It is threads, hundreds of tiny threads which sew people together through the years." – **Simone Signoret**

"Happy marriages begin when we marry the ones we love, and they blossom when we love the ones we marry." – **Tom Mullen**

"Love at first sight is easy to understand; it's when two people have been looking at each other for a lifetime that it becomes a miracle." – **Sam Levenson**

"Sexiness wears thin after a while and beauty fades, but to be married to a man who makes you laugh every day, ah, now that's a real treat." – **Joanne Woodward**

"A great marriage is not when the *'perfect couple'* come together. It is when an imperfect couple learns to enjoy their differences." – **Dave Meur**

"It is not a lack of love, but a lack of friendship that makes unhappy marriages." – **Friedrich Nietzsche**

"The great secret of successful marriage is to treat all disasters as incidents and none of the incidents as disasters." – **Sir Harold George Nicolson**

"Love never gives up, never loses faith, is always hopeful, and endures through every circumstance." – **I Corinthians 13:7**

"What counts in making a happy marriage is not so much how compatible you are, but how you deal with incompatibility." – **Leo Tolstoy**

"Before you marry a person, you should first make them use a computer with slow Internet to see who they really are." – **Will Ferrell**

"There is no remedy for love but to love more." – **Henry David Thoreau**

"When a wife has a good husband, it is easily seen in her face." – **Goethe**

"A happy marriage is the union of two good forgivers." – **Robert Quillen**

"I didn't marry you because you were perfect. I didn't even marry you because I loved you. I married you because you gave me a promise. That promise made up for your faults. And the promise I gave you made up for mine." Source unknown

"Two imperfect people got married and it was the promise that made the marriage. And when our children were growing up, it wasn't a house that protected them; and it wasn't our love that protected them – it was that promise." – **Thornton Wilder**

"The goal in marriage is not to think alike, but to think together." – **Robert C. Dodds**

"Marriage is our last, best chance to grow up." – **Joseph Barth**

"Love is not something you feel. It is something you do." – **David Wilkerson**

"There is nothing nobler or more admirable than when two people who see eye to eye, keep house as man and wife, confounding their enemies and delighting their friends." – **Homer**

"I got gaps; you got gaps; we fill each other's gaps." – **Rocky**

"You come to love not by finding the right person, but by seeing an imperfect person perfectly." – **Sam Keen**

"You make me happier than I ever thought I could be and if you let me I will spend the rest of my life trying to make you feel the same way." – **Chandler proposing**

"Marriage success cannot always be ascribed to the presence of communication, but marriage failure can be traced to the absence of communication." – **Deji Badiru**

"When a man steals your wife, there is no better revenge than to let him keep her." **Lee Majors**

"After marriage, husband and wife become two sides of a coin; they just can't face each other, but still they stay together." **Al Gore**

"The great question... which I have not been able to answer... is, 'What does a woman want?'"
George Clooney

"I had some words with my wife, and she had some paragraphs with me." **Bill Clinton**

"Some people ask the secret of our long marriage. We take time to go to a restaurant two times a week. A little candlelight, dinner, soft music and dancing. She goes Tuesdays, I go Fridays."
George W. Bush

"I don't worry about terrorism. I was married for two years." **Rudy Giuliani**

"There's a way of transferring funds that is even faster than electronic banking. It's called marriage." **Michael Jordan**

"I've had bad luck with all my wives. The first one left me and the second one didn't. The third gave me more children!" **Donald Trump**

"Two secrets to keep your marriage brimming

1. Whenever you're wrong, admit it,
2. Whenever you're right, shut up." **Shaquille O'Neal**

"The most effective way to remember your wife's birthday is to forget it once..." **Kobe Bryant**

"You know what I did before I married? Anything I wanted to." **David Hasselhoff**

"The best salutation to a newly-wed man is 'Welcome to the loss of freedom.'" **Deji Badiru**

"My wife and I were happy for twenty years. Then we met." **Alec Baldwin**

"A good wife always forgives her husband when she's wrong." **Barack Obama**

"Marriage is the only war where one sleeps with the enemy." **Tommy Lee**

"A man inserted an 'ad' in the classifieds: "Wife wanted". Next day he received a hundred letters. They all said the same thing: "You can have mine." **Brad Pitt**

"First Guy (proudly): "My wife's an angel!"
Second Guy: "You're lucky, mine's still alive." **Jimmy Kimmel**

"Honey, what happened to 'ladies first'?" Husband replies, "That's the reason why the world's a mess today, because a lady went first!" **David Letterman**

"First there's the promise ring, then the engagement ring, then the wedding ring...soon after....comes Suffer...ing! **Jay Leno**

On the Attributes of a Wife

* When she is quiet, millions of things are running in her mind.
* When she stares at you, she is wondering why she loves you so much in spite of being taken for granted.
* When she says I will stand by you, she will stand by you like a rock.

Never hurt her or take her wrong or for granted...

A joke from the home front

"If your wife is sick, don't rush her to the hospital immediately, send money to her account first, if she doesn't get well immediately then you can take her to the hospital. We just found out there is a new sickness common among wives called money'laria and it is worse than malaria. The best treatment for it is a bank deposit alert." Source unknown

"They argue most who are married the longest." – Deji Badiru

This is because they have seen the most of things together. Each cannot pull the wool over the eyes of the other.

Jerry, we should turn left at this junction.
No, Joan, right is the right way to turn. So, goes a typical argument between a long-married couple.

"I recently read that love is entirely a matter of chemistry. That must be why my wife treats me like toxic waste."

- David Bissonette

"When a man steals your wife, there is no better revenge than to let him keep her."

- Sacha Guitry"After marriage, husband and wife become two sides of a coin; they just can't face each other, but still they stay together."

- Hemant Joshi"By all means marry. If you get a good wife, you'll be happy. If you get a bad one, you'll become a philosopher."

- Socrates"Woman inspires us to great things, and prevents us from achieving them."

- Dumas

"The great question... which I have not been able to answer... is, 'What does a woman want?'"

- Sigmund Freud

"I had some words with my wife, and she had some paragraphs with me."

- Anonymous"Some people ask the secret of our long marriage. We take time to go to a restaurant two times a week. A little candlelight, dinner, soft music and dancing. She goes Tuesdays, I go Fridays."

- Henny Youngman"I don't worry about terrorism. I was married for two years."

- Sam Kinison"There's a way of transferring funds that is even faster than electronic banking. It's called marriage."

- James Holt McGavran"I've had bad luck with both my wives. The first one left me, and the second one didn't."

- Patrick Murray

"Two secrets to keep your marriage brimming:1. Whenever you're wrong, admit it,2. Whenever you're right, shut up."

- Nash"The most effective way to remember your wife's birthday is to forget it once."

- Anonymous

"You may forget your wife's age, but don't forget the birthday."

- Deji Badiru

"You know what I did before I married? Anything I wanted to."

- Henny Youngman"My wife and I were happy for twenty years. Then we met."

- Rodney Dangerfield"A good wife always forgives her husband when she's wrong."

- Milton Berle"Marriage is the only war where one sleeps with the enemy."

- Anonymous"A man inserted an 'ad' in the classifieds: 'Wife wanted'. Next day he received a hundred letters. They all said the same thing: 'You can have mine.'"

- AnonymousFirst Guy (proudly): 'My wife's an angel!'Second Guy: 'You are lucky. Mine is still alive.'

- Source unknown

Question: Why would a man want to go to the moon, so far away?
Answer: To get away from the wife.

"Spouses and spats spice up a home." – Deji Badiru

"Marriage is an act of will that signifies and involves a mutual gift, which unites the spouses and binds them to their eventual souls, with whom they make up a sole family - a domestic church."

- Pope John Paul II

"Speak with words that are soft and sweet; you never know which ones you may have to eat."

- American Cowboy Saying

Parody of Wife's Work

Conversation between a husband and a Counselor:C: What do you do for a living Mr. Bandy?H: I work as an Accountant in a Bank.C: What about your Wife?H: She doesn't work. She's a Housewife only.C: Who makes breakfast for your family in the morning?H : My Wife, because she doesn't work.C: At what time does your wife wake up for making breakfast?H: She wakes up at around 5 am because she cleans the house first before making breakfast.C: How do your kids go to school?H: My wife takes them to school, because she doesn't work.C: After taking your kids to school, what does she do?H: She goes to the market, then goes back home for cooking and laundry. You know, she doesn't work.C: In the evening, after you go back home from office, what do you do?H : Take rest, because I'm tired due to all-day work.C: What does your wife do then?H: She prepares meals, serving our kids, preparing meals for me and cleaning the dishes, cleaning the house then taking kids to bed. The moral of the parody: Appreciate your wives because of their immense support, commitment, and sacrifices.Hail to Wives!

CHAPTER FIVE

Intellectual Tribute: Case Example of Einstein's Wife

Some items that are being historically reported about Albert Einstein's wife are quite fascinating. As a scholar myself, I am very intrigued by piecing together the pieces of information about Einstein's wife. History often presents different views and accounts of long-ago events. Not much is often heard about Einstein's wife. Some believe she was as brilliant as Einstein, if not better. But why is much not heard about her? By contrast, much is known about Marie Currie because she was the first woman to win a Nobel Prize. The first person and only woman to win it twice and the only person to win a Nobel Prize in two different sciences, physics and chemistry.

What about Mileva Maric-Einstein, Albert Einstein's wife? Where and what is her history? She was the only woman in the Physics department at Zurich Polytechnic when Albert Einstein studied there. In fact, it was reported that she was the only person to score higher than Einstein in mathematics at the entrance exam. What was the historical difference between Marie Currie and Mileva Maric-Einstein? Why did one go down in history as a great scientist with two Nobel Prizes while the other is known just as Albert Einstein's wife?

Mileva Marić-Einstein got married to Einstein and helped him in writing some of the most profound papers that changed science but Einstein never cited her in his works, so it was reported. This might have been a sign of the time for that era.

Maria Curie married Pierre Curie, a man who demonstrated spousal partnership. When the Nobel Prize committee wrote Pierre Curie in 1903 informing him that he had won the Nobel Prize, Pierre asked if his wife was also going to be honored, but he was told only him and Henri Becquerel would be honored. Pierre wrote the Nobel Prize committee acknowledging the honor, but rejecting it if his wife would not be honored. He said the papers had a heavy input from his wife. The committee budged and Marie Currie became the first woman to win a Nobel Prize.

Albert Einstein, on the other hand, didn't consider to put Maric's name on his publications. Such actions would later cause controversy in the scientific world, which still leads to debates nowadays on Maric's contributions. The moral of this story, a proper wifely credit where and when needed can shape the course of historical legacy. Talking of collateral legacy, the eldest daughter of Pierre and Marie Curie, Irene Joliot Curie, with her husband, Frederic Joliot became joint winners of the Nobel Prize in Chemistry in 1935. That is thirty-two years after Pierre and Marie accomplished the feat together in 1903. Spousal credit matters!

Concluding remarks

Wives matter a great deal. Through the medium of this comically book, I hope you have enjoyed some of the renditions of life through the eyes of wives and husbands. May the union remain strong.

CHAPTER SIX

Household Conversion Reference for Wives and Husbands

```
1 pinch ............................…....…..... 1/8 tea spoon or less
3 tea spoons.............................…..…..... 1 table spoon
2 table spoons...............................…..…..... 1/8 cup
4 table spoons...............................…...…............1/4 cup
8 table spoons...........................................1/2 cup
12 table spoons..........................................3/4 cup
16 table spoons..............…...........................…. 1 cup
5 table spoons + 1 tea spoon....................…....... 1/3 cup
4 oz...........…...............................…...... 1/2 cup
8oz...................................…..........…...... 1 cup
16 oz .........................................…...…...... 1 lb
1 oz...............................…....2 table spoons fat or liquid
1 cup of liquid..........................…....…..............1/2 pint
2 cups.............................…...............…...…..... 1 pint
2 pints..............................…...…................ 1 quart
4 cup of liquid............................…...…...........1 quart
4 quarts......…..............…...…...................…........ 1 gallon
8 quarts...….............….... 1 peck (such as apples, pears, etc.)
1 jigger.............…...….........................1 ½ fluid oz
1 jigger...........…...…......................... .3 table spoons
```

Notation	Expansion
yotta (10^{24}):w	1, 000, 000, 000, 000, 000, 000, 000, 000
zetta (10^{21}):	1, 000, 000, 000, 00,0 000, 000, 000
exa (10^{18}):	1, 000, 000, 000, 000, 000, 000
peta (10^{15}):	1, 000, 000, 000, 000, 000
tera (10^{12}):	1, 000, 000, 000, 000
giga (10^{9}):	1, 000, 000, 000
mega (10^{6}):	1, 000, 000
kilo (10^{3}):	1, 000
hecto (10^{2}):	100
deca (10^{1}):	10
deci (10^{-1}):	0.1
centi (10^{-2}):	0.01
milli (10^{-3}):	0.001
micro (10^{-6}):	0.000 001
nano (10^{-9}):	0.000 000 001
pico (10^{-12}):	0.000 000 000 001
femto (10^{-15}):	0.000 000 000 000 001
atto (10^{-18}):	0.000 000 000 000 000 001
zepto (10^{-21}):	0.000 000 000 000 000 000 001
yocto (10^{-24}):	0.000 000 000 000 000 000 000 001
stringo (10^{-35}):	0.000 000 000 000 000 000 000 000 000 000 01

English system		
1 foot (ft)	= 12 inches (in) 1'=12"	in
1 yard (yd)	= 3 feet	ft
1 mile (mi)	= 1760 yards	yd
1 sq. foot	= 144 sq. inches	sq in
1 sq. yard	= 9 sq. feet	sq ft
1 acre	= 4840 sq. yards = 43560 ft^2	sq yd
1 sq. mile	= 640 acres	acres
Metric system		
mm	millimeter	.001 m
cm	centimeter	.01 m
dm	decimeter	.1 m
m	meter	1 m
dam	decameter	10 m
hm	hectometer	100 m
km	kilometer	1000 m

Multiply	by	to obtain
angstrom	10^{-10}	meters
feet	0.30480	meters
	12	inches
inches	25.40	millimeters
	0.02540	meters
	0.08333	feet
kilometers	3280.8	feet
	0.6214	miles
	1094	yards
meters	39.370	inches
	3.2808	feet
	1.094	yards
miles	5280	feet
	1.6093	kilometers
	0.8694	nautical miles
millimeters	0.03937	inches
nautical miles	6076	feet
	1.852	kilometers
yards	0.9144	meters
	3	feet
	36	inches

Multiply	by	to obtain
feet/minute	5.080	mm/second
feet/second	0.3048	meters/second
inches/second	0.0254	meters/second
km/hour	0.6214	miles/hour
meters/second	3.2808	feet/second
	2.237	miles/hour
miles/hour	88.0	feet/minute
	0.44704	meters/second
	1.6093	km/hour
	0.8684	knots
knot	1.151	miles/hour

Multiply	by	to obtain
carat	0.200	cubic grams
grams	0.03527	ounces
kilograms	2.2046	pounds
ounces	28.350	grams
pound	16	ounces
	453.6	grams
stone (UK)	6.35	kilograms
	14	pounds
ton (net)	907.2	kilograms
	2000	pounds
	0.893	gross tons
	0.907	metric tons
ton (gross)	2240	pounds
	1.12	net tons
	1.016	metric tons
tonne (metric)	2,204.623	pounds
	0.984	gross pound
	1000	kilograms

Multiply	By	To Obtain
acres	43,560	sq feet
	4,047	sq meters
	4,840	sq yards
	0.405	hectare
sq cm	0.155	sq inches
sq feet	144	sq inches
	0.09290	sq meters
	0.1111	sq yards
sq inches	645.16	sq millimeters
sq kilometers	0.3861	sq miles
sq meters	10.764	sq feet
	1.196	sq yards
sq miles	640	acres
	2.590	sq kilometers

144 square inches = 1 square foot
9 square feet = 1 square yard
43,560 square feet = 1 acre
640 acres = 1 square mile
30-1/4 square yards = 1 square rod
40 square rods = 1 square rood
4 square roods = 1 acre
272-1/4 square feet = 1 square rod

Multiply	by	to obtain
acre-foot	1233.5	cubic meters
cubic cm	0.06102	cubic inches
cubic feet	1728	cubic inches
	7.480	gallons (US)
	0.02832	cubic meters
	0.03704	cubic yards
liter	1.057	liquid quarts
	0.908	dry quarts
	61.024	cubic inches
gallons (US)	231	cubic inches
	3.7854	liters
	4	quarts
	0.833	British gallons
	128 U.S.	fluid ounces
quarts (US)	0.9463	liters

Multiply	by	to obtain
BTU	1055.9	joules
	0.2520	kg-calories
watt-hour	3600	joules
	3.409	BTU
HP (electric)	746	watts
BTU/second	1055.9	watts
watt-second	1.00	joules

Celsius to Kelvin	$K = C + 273.15$
Celsius to Fahrenheit	$F = (9/5)C + 32$
Fahrenheit to Celsius	$C = (5/9)(F - 32)$
Fahrenheit to Kelvin	$K = (5/9)(F + 459.67)$
Fahrenheit to Rankin	$R = F + 459.67$
Rankin to Kelvin	$K = (5/9)R$

Multiply	by	to obtain
atmospheres	1.01325	bars
	33.90	feet of water
	29.92	inches of mercury
	760.0	mm of mercury
bar	75.01	cm of mercury
	14.50	pounds/sq inch
dyne/sq cm	0.1	N/sq meter
newtons/sq cm	1.450	pounds/sq inch
pounds/sq inch	0.06805	atmospheres
	2.036	inches of mercury
	27.708	inches of water
	68.948	millibars
	51.72	mm of mercury

Speed of light	$2.997,925 \times 10^{10}$ cm/sec
	983.6×10^6 ft/sec
	186,284 miles/sec
Velocity of sound	340.3 meters/sec
	1116 ft/sec
	1116 ft/sec
Gravity (acceleration)	9.80665 m/sec square
	32.174 ft/sec square
	386.089 inches/sec square

12 inches = 1 foot

3 feet = 1 yard

5-1/2 yards = 1 rod

6 feet = 1 fathom

40 rods = 1 furlong

8 furlongs = 1 mile

1760 yards = 1 mile

5280 feet = 1 mile

60 sea miles = 1 degree

0.8684 miles = 1 sea mile1 radian = 57.3°

1 inch	= 2.54 cm
1 gallon	= 231 in^3
1 kilogram	= 2.205 lb
1 newton	= 1 kg•m/s^2
1 joule	= 1 N•m
1 watt	= 1 J/s
1 pascal	= 1 N/m^2
1 BTU	= 778 ft-lb
	= 252 cal
	= 1,054.8 J
1 horsepower	= 745.7 W
1 atmosphere	= 14.7 lb/in^2
	= 1.01•10^5 N/m^2

Liquid Measure	Dry Measure
4 gills = 1 pint	2 pints = 1 quart
2 pints = 1 quart	8 quarts = 1 peck
4 quart = 1 gallon	4 pecks = 1 bushel
31-1/2 gallons = 1 barrel	36 bushels = 1 chaldron
231 cu. In. = 1 gallon	2,150.42 cu. In. = 1 standard bushel
	1 cubic foot = approx. 4/5 bushel

Printed in the United States
By Bookmasters